St. Andrew, the Patron Saint of Scotland

ST. ANDREW,

THE

PATRON SAINT OF SCOTLAND.

—BY—

HON. THOMAS L. TULLOCK.

FROM THE GRANITE MONTHLY,
APRIL, 1882.

CONCORD, N. H.:
PRINTED BY EVANS & SLEEPER,
1882.

SAINT ANDREW,

THE PATRON SAINT OF SCOTLAND.

I N accordance with a time-honored and much cherished custom, the Saint Andrew's Society of Washington, assembles annually, on the evening of the 30th of November, to celebrate the festival of St Andrew, the Patron Saint of Scotland This anniversary has, with few exceptions, been regularly commemorated by the Society since its organization. The meetings have uniformly been characterized by good cheer and fraternal greetings, and have proved profitable as well as agreeable reunions of the Sons of Auld Scotia, whose homes are in this beautiful Capital of our nation Thus are revived recollections of old friendships, while new ones are created and cemented , and thus, too, above all, is kept alive and strengthened our love for both our native land and our adopted country, while to us of Scotch lineage only, is renewed and refreshed our interest in our ancestral home

After a thorough research of authorities for information relating to the eventful life and exalted character of so distinguished a personage as St Andrew, I have to regret the limited record concerning him The commemoration of the anniversary of the Apostle's death, as a national holiday and festival, by the Scottish people, was no doubt first observed by them in the year 359, and from that time to the present it has been generally celebrated in Scotland as the great religious and social festival of the nation And on this their gala-day, the 30th of November, Scotchmen wherever congregated revive the memories of the past, and with appropriate festivities celebrate this time-honored anniversary

Upon what appears to be equally reliable authority, St Andrew was admitted into the Masonic Calendar, on the 30th of November, 1737, when his anniversary was adopted by the fraternity as an annual festival also, and that day is now everywhere recognized by the brethren of the mystic tie There are some who contend that the festival of St Andrew was placed at the head of the holidays beginning at Advent, from the circumstance of his having been the first who found the Saviour, as well as the first who brought others to Him In the Book of Common Prayer, are the Collect, Epistle and Gospel appointed by the church specially for St Andrew's day In the niches of the ecclesiastical year devoted to eminent saints, this Apostle has a prominent place For centuries all who kept Saint's days have publicly assembled to celebrate his name and work.

Other countries than Scotland have their tutelar Saints. England honors St. George, who is represented on horseback, clad in full armor with a vanquished dragon at his feet. Ireland patronises St. Patrick; while the guardian saint of Spain is St. James; of France, St. Denis; of Italy, St. Anthony; and of Wales, St. David. The patron Saints of Genoa, are St. George, St. Lawrence and St. John the Baptist. On the piazzetta at Venice, their are two granite columns, one bearing the "Winged Lion of St. Mark," the emblem of the tutelary Saint of Venice; the other, St. Theodore on a crocodile, the patron of the ancient Republic. St. Michael is regarded as the patron or guardian angel of the Jews.

But this is a degression. I will not test your patience by reference to other celebrities, but proceed at once to present the historical and legendary account of our own revered patron Saint, who is also the patron of Russia, Hungary and Burgundy. In this effort to throw some new light upon the history of St. Andrew, and to illustrate his character, I shall necessarily blend to a very large extent, the authentic record of Scripture with statements which rest alone on tradition.

Without elaborately quoting authorities, or citing passages of Scripture which refer to St. Andrew or his ministry, I have to say that his name signifies manly, and is of Greek origin : *aner—aneros*, or *andros*—man. He was one of the twelve Apostles who were commissioned to preach the Gospel, and appears as one of the confidential disciples who accompanied the Saviour in his earthly mission. He was born in Bethsaida, a town in Galilee, situated on the shore of Lake Tiberias, in Palestine, and near the head at its northern extremity. The country adjacent abounded in deer, and the sea in fish, and therefore hunting and fishing were both the pastime and occupation of many of its inhabitants. To this locality Jesus frequently resorted. Andrew was a younger brother of Simon Peter. Their father's name was Jonas, and the vocation of himself and sons was that of fishermen. Being a disciple of St. John the Baptist, who at the fords of the Jordan had expressly designated Jesus as the Lamb of God, Andrew was led to receive Him as the Messiah, and was distinguished as the "First Called" of the disciples, and to the Master he brought his brother Simon, afterwards called Peter, and hence is named by some of the fathers as "The Rock before the Rock." Neither of them, however, became at that time the stated attendants on our Lord. Pursuing their humble occupation as fishermen, they were not called by Jesus to follow Him, until after the imprisonment of John. This was about twelve months after Simon's introduction to Christ. Then Andrew and Peter, together with James and John, were personally called by our Lord when passing through Galilee. Finding them fishing upon the sea of Tiberias, he gave them a miraculous draught of fishes, thereby demonstrating his divine power. They left their nets and followed Him. The employment of most of the twelve Apostles, if not of all of them, with the exception of Matthew, a tax-gatherer, was probably the laborious occupation of fishermen. Paul was a tent-maker.

The principal incidents mentioned in the Gospels, in which St. Andrew's name occurs during the life of Christ, are the feeding of the five thousand. It was Andrew who said, "There is a lad here, which hath five barley loaves and two small fishes." His introduction to our Lord at Jerusalem, during the Passover week, of certain Greeks who desired to see Him, which, together with his having brought his brother Peter to the Saviour after announcing to him "we have found the Messiah," caused him to be called the "Introducer to Christ." Another incident was his asking with other disciples, Peter, John and James, for a further explanation of what our Lord had said in reference to the destruction of the Temple. Andrew was with St. John the

Baptist, the day following the baptism of Jesus, when our Lord was saluted by John, who exclaimed, " Behold the Lamb of God," and Andrew followed Him. He was also present with the mother of Jesus and with the other disciples, at the marriage in Cana of Galilee, and witnessed the miracle there wrought by the Saviour After they were called by Jesus while fishing in the lake, and were made "fishers of men," Andrew and his brother Peter were regular in their attendance upon Him, and in the prosecution of their new mission Andrew received the evidence of Christ's resurrection from Mary Magdelene and the other women who had visited the tomb, and he saw Him and heard His voice when He said " Peace be unto you " He was also at Olivet on the ascension morning, and with others received the Saviour's blessing • Andrew and Peter after becoming disciples left " Bethsaida, the city of Andrew and Peter," and lived in Capernaum It was at their house that Jesus lodged when He preached in that city, and it was also at their house and at the request of both, that He cured Peter's wife's mother of a fever   •

It appears that from Christ's disciples who had listened to His matchless teachings and witnessed the miracles proving His Messiahship, and were thereby qualified to give reliable testimony concerning Him, that He chose His Apostles In enumerating them, two of the evangelists mention first the names of the two brothers. Connected with the Apostle's creed, which is so universally adopted by the Greek, Roman and Protestant churches, and so generally believed as a summary of Christian faith, there is a legend, that the creed was composed by the Apostles at Jerusalem before their separation after the day of Pentecost, each one contributing a sentence for the purpose of securing unity of teaching in the great outline of the faith they professed The creed consists of twelve articles, and to Peter are ascribed the words " I believe in God, the Father Almighty " To Andrew, " and in Jesus Christ, his only son, our Lord," and to John, " Suffered under Pontius Pilate." The words attributed to Andrew are by some credited to John, while the article ascribed to John is named as originating with Andrew, while another writer concedes to Andrew the sentence, " who was conceived by the Holy Ghost, born of the Virgin Mary "

After our Lord's ascension, when the Apostles were miraculously endowed and qualified for their sacred mission, the vast northern region of Scythia and Sogdiana and the neighboring countries was assigned to Andrew, who traversed those inhospitable regions upon the dispersion of the Apostles, encountering hazards most perilous with an unflinching courage and a pious determination, which could only have been inspired by the blessed hope he cherished Concerning St Andrew's ministry, Origen writes that he preached at Scythia, (Russia) St Jerome, also Eusebius, says he preached at Achaia (Greece), Nicophorus, in Asia Minor and Thrace (Turkey in Europe) , St Paulinus names Argos, where the Apostle preached, silencing their philosophers Other ancient writers name other places as having been visited by him, as Sogdiana, Colchis and Epirus Tradition particularly assigns as the scenes of his ministry, Russia, Greece, Asia Minor and Turkey in Europe, which may be regarded as the field of his Apostolic labor Other localities are named where he zealously propagated the doctrines of Christianity and confirmed his teachings by miracles At Synope on the Euxine (Black) sea, he was maltreated and suffered great cruelties The inhabitants became exasperated against him, and conspired to burn the house in which he lodged, which design was frustrated They, however, treated him with savage cruelty, throwing him to the ground, stamping upon him, pulling and dragging him from place to place. He was beaten with clubs, pelted with stones, and there were some so demonical and brutish as to be guilty of biting off his flesh with their teeth.

When supposed to be entirely deprived of life, he was cast aside into a field as dead. But he miraculously recovered and returned publicly to the city, where he recommenced his labors and wrought miracles. He was eminently successful. Many believed his teachings and were converted, and became of like precious faith with himself. An author quoting from the ancients, says that while at this place, Andrew met his brother Peter, and they both remained at Synope for some time. The chairs, made of white stone, wherein they were accustomed to sit when instructing the people, were existing and commonly shown in his time. Andrew afterwards returned to Jerusalem, and from thence travelled extensively, encountering many difficulties and great hardships until his execution.

It is believed that he established a church in Byzantium (Constantinople), and ordained Stachys, who had been named by Paul as its first Bishop, and alluded to in his epistles to the Romans as "My beloved." He was bishop sixteen years. Andrew's travels may be succinctly enumerated by stating that after leaving Jerusalem, he first journeyed through Cappadocia, Galatia and Bithynia, provinces of Asia Minor, continuing along the Euxine Sea, into the desert of Scythia. An ancient author writes that he first came to Amynsus, where he preached in one of the Jewish Synagogues, next to Trapazium, a maritime city on the Euxine Sea, thence after visiting other places he came to Nice in Northern Italy, where he remained two years; then passed to Niesmedia and Chalcedon, whence he sailed through the Propontis to the Euxine again, and from there to Heraclen, and afterwards to Amastres and thence to Synope. Returning to Jerusalem, from thence he travelled over Thrace, Macedonia, Thessera, Achaia and Epirus, until he came to Patras, a city of Achaia in Greece, where his earthly mission ended, after a very laborious and perilous service, which he resolutely conducted with constancy and fidelity. The Muscovites claim that St. Andrew carried the Gospel into their country "as far as the mouth of the Borysthenes," in Russia, and "to the mountains where the city of Kiow now stands, to the frontiers of Poland." They believe that he was the first to preach to the Slavonians in Novogorod, also in Sarmatia, the vast region of Eastern Europe and Western Asia, which includes the most considerable portion of Poland, and the whole of Central and Southern Russia, except the Crimea and Northern Hungary.

They honor him as the principal titular saint of the Empire. Peter the Great created under Andrew's name, the first as well as the most noble order of knighthood,—the Knight of the Blue Ribbon, December 20, 1698,—in commemoration of the supposed introduction of Christianity in the Russian Empire, by the Apostle Andrew. This order is the highest in rank in the Empire, and is confined to members of the Imperial family, princes and the chief officers of the realm, being only bestowed by special favor of the Emperor. The badge or medal is the figure of St. Andrew on a gold enamelled cross, on the corners of which are four letters S. A. P. R., "Sanctius Andreas Patronus Russae." On the reverse is the Imperial Eagle with spread wings and double-headed, with the legend, in Russian, "For religion and loyality," and the name of the Saint. It is fastened to a sky blue ribbon and suspended from the right shoulder towards the left hip, but at festivals is pendant to a collar of gold, composed of square chains and roses. The collar of the order consists of St. Andrew crosses alternating with imperial crowns. The Emperors carry a St. Andrew's cross with the figure of the Apostle with a smaller cross. Beneath and above may be defined the double-headed emblematic eagle, with an inscription, "Peter possessor and autocrat of Russia." The decorations have undergone some alterations since the Order of St. Andrew was instituted, but the Apostle and his cross have always been the conspicious jewel—studded with diamonds The Russian naval flag is distinguished by a purple St Andrew cross on a white ground, another indication of their reverence for his memory

One of the historians of Scotland (Cullen) says "There is little doubt but Christianity was promulgated very early in Britain, that St Paul personally preached in the island, and that the gospel was preached in Scotland by St Andrew the Apostle." Christianity was in a flourishing state in Scotland at the beginning of the fourth century, when the tenth and last persecution of the Christians under Dioclesian raged most furiously Many of the British Christians fled for refuge to Scotland The sanguinary persecutions commenced A. D. 303 and lasted ten years It was in this persecution that St George, the Patron of England suffered martyrdom Having mentioned the countries recorded as having been visited by St Andrew, the termination of his public ministry is reached He suffered martyrdom, being crucified at Patras, in Achaia, in Greece, by order of Aegeas, the Roman pro-consul, who, enraged by his preaching, commanded him to join in sacrifices to the heathen gods, and upon his refusal, ordered him to be severely scourged and then crucified, a sentence which was executed with peculiar cruelty,—seven lictors alternately exerting their strength with the scourge on the Apostle's shoulders To make his death the more lingering, he was fastened to the cross with cords, instead of the customary nails He survived the terrible torture two days, and while strength endured, praised God and exhorted those who witnessed his sufferings to repentance and faith—teaching and instructing them in the way of life He welcomed the cross and the martyr's crown, and exultantly accepted the fate that awaited him Great interest was manifested to spare his life, but the Apostle earnestly desired to depart, and to seal with his blood, the truth of the religion he professed His body is said to have been embalmed and honorably intombed by Maximilla, who had embraced the Christian religion,—a lady of "quality and estate," believed to be the wife of the pro-consul who had caused his death

Patras is described as a "city seated on a hill, near the sea" It is a fortified seaport in Greece, on the Gulf of Patras, and the principal entry of its foreign trade "One of its churches is traditionally connected with the martyrdom of St Andrew, and is greatly resorted to by devotees" In ancient times the goddess Diana was worshipped at Patras The cruel custom of sacrificing to her yearly, "a most beautiful young man and maid," was continued until by the preaching of St Andrew, Eusypilus was converted to Christianity, when that wicked superstition ceased

The account of the Apostle's martyrdom is given in the "Acts of his Passion,"—said to have been written by the presbyters and deacons of Achaia, present at the time—a work of great antiquity, being mentioned by Philastrius about 380 The Apostle had been eminently successful in his mission Multitudes had fallen off from paganism and embraced the Christian faith, among whom are mentioned the pro-consul's wife (Maximilla) and his brother (Stratocles), which caused Aegeas great rage and displeasure, and hence his cruel treatment of the Apostle

The cross on which the Apostle was suspended, was made of two pieces of timber crossing each other obliquely in the centre in the form of the letter X, "crus decussata," and from this the St Andrew's cross derived its name It is supposed that the Apostle expired on the 30th day of November, in the year 69 His remains were afterwards removed to Constantinople by Constantine the Great, and buried with great solemnity in the great church he had erected in honor of the Apostles, where they remained till the year 369, when it is said an Abbot, named Regulus, who was a pious Greek devotee, caused them to be removed to Scotland, or at least certain relics of the Saint; said to be the arm bone, three fingers of the right hand and three toes, and deposited them in the church, with a monastery which he erected to the memory of St Andrew at Abernethy, where now is established the city of St Andrew, in the county of Fife, with its far famed University, the most ancient of the four Scottish Universities, and believed to be the only one in Europe where theology is the sole study The city originated from the Abbey, which was in a flourishing condition when the University of St Andrew was founded, about the year 1411 It was to this church of St Regulus, that pilgrims from foreign countries resorted in the early ages "Hungas, King of the Picts," about the year 809, in acknowledgment for great success which he had achieved in battle, gave to this church the See of Kilrule, the tenth part of his dominion, and directed that the cross of St Andrew should thenceforth be the badge of the country Kenneth II, King of the Scots, having conquered the Picts, whose capital was at Abernethy, extinguished their kingdom in North Britain in 845, and transferred the seat of government from Abernethy to the town of Kilrule, changing its name to St Andrew, and ordering that the Bishop of St Andrew should be the chief in the kingdom He also "repaired and richly endowed the church of St Regulus, in which the arm of St. Andrew was reverently kept"

According to an ancient legend or tradition, it is pretended that Hungas, who reigned over the Picts in Scotland in the 9th century, had a vision (833) the night preceding one of his battles, in which the Apostle Andrew appeared and promised to him a decisive victory, assuring him that a token or a sign should appear over the Pictish host, representing a cross fashioned as the one upon which St Andrew suffered Hungas, awaking, looked up to the sky, and saw the promised cross, as did all of both armies The vision when related greatly encouraged the Picts, and the appearance of the cross terrified the army of King Athelstan, who was killed in the ensuing battle After achieving victory, Hungas, to express his thankfulness for prevailing over the King of the ancient Saxons, went in solemn procession to the Kirk of St. Andrew, to render thanks to God and His Apostle for the victory, and with the Picts on that occasion vowed for themselves and their posterity, that from henceforth in time of war, they should wear as a badge of cognizance the cross of St Andrew Hungas as a further expression of thankfulness, gave to the church of Regulus divers rich gifts, including many to adorn the church, and also "a case of beaten gold for preserving the relics of St Andrew" John Leslie, Bishop of Ross, Scotland, says that the cross of St Andrew "appeared to Achaius, King of the Scots, and Hungas, King of the Picts, the night before the battle was fought betwixt them and Athelstane, King of England, as they were on their knees in prayer"

The See of St Andrew was established in 518, and the city of St Andrew, became the seat of the Scottish primacy, and therefore the ecclesiastical metropolis of the kingdom The origin of the city was in the very early period I have named. The legend concerning it, is that Regulus, the Greek monk of Patrae in Achaia, about the year 370, was commanded by a vision from heaven to leave his own country for the island of Albion, the ancient name of Great Britain, and there preach the gospel to the Picts Having passed through the Mediterranean, and coasted along the shores of Spain and France, he entered the German Ocean, where after a tedious and tempestuous passage, he was shipwrecked in the Bay now called St Andrew, and with difficulty reached the shore, accompanied by his companions, a few monks, and the small box which contained the relics of the Apostle Andrew Hergustus, who was then King of the Picts, received the strangers graciously, and in a short time em-

braced the Christian religion, as did a great part of his subjects. He afterwards presented St. Regulus with one of his palaces and some lands, and built
him a church, of which the ruins still exist at St. Andrew, bearing the
name of Regulus. The companions of Regulus are named as Damianus, a
priest, Gelasius, Tubaculus and Mermacus, deacons, Nerinus and Elisenius,
a Cretian, Merinus and Silvaneus his brother, monks by profession, and eight
other persons, five hermits and three devoted virgins. Regulus lived here
thirty-two years, and established the first Christian priests of the country called
Culdees, signifying "God's servants." They were generally married men—
pious and indefatigable, and respected for their zeal and virtues. Regulus
changed the name of the church and place from Kilrymout to Kilrule.

Kenneth to whom reference has been made as having translated the Episco-
pal See which the Picts had established at Abernethy, to St. Andrew, died in
854. As an item of Scottish history, I will mention that the marble stone
which Fergus, the first King of Scotland, had placed at Argyle about 330 years
before the Christian era, Kenneth caused to be removed to Scone, by the river
Tay, about two miles north of Perth, and had it enclosed in a wooden chair in
which the Kings of Scotland were afterwards crowned. It was removed to
England by King Edward I., in 1297, together with the Scotch sceptre and crown.
This famous stone was originally brought from Spain to Ireland, from whence
Fergus came, and had been preserved at Argyle and Scone for many centuries.
It is claimed by some, as being the veritable Jacob's Pillow, brought to
Ireland by the prophet Jeremiah, afterwards known as St. Patriarch or St. Patrick.
It is quite a large marble block fitted in the chair, below the seat, and is fully
exposed to view. It is now in the Chapel of St. Edward, in Westminister
Abbey, and is known as the coronation chair in which all the reigning sover-
eigns of England have been crowned since Edward the First. When in
London in 1873, I had the privilege of inspecting this ancient relic.

In the records of the duchy of Burgundy it is mentioned that the cross of
St. Andrew, made of Olive wood, was removed from Achaia, the place of the
Apostle's crucifixion, and deposited in a nunnery at Weaune, near Marseilles;
but was lost during the Moorish invasion, and subsequently rediscovered by
Hugues, a monk, and placed in the Abbey of St. Victor in Marseilles in the year
1250, where it is now venerated. A part thereof enclosed in "a silver case,
gilt," was carried to Brussels in 1433, by Philip the Good, Duke of Burgundy,
who obtained at great cost "the precious relic." In honor of it he instituted
his famous order of chivalry, known as the "Knights of the Golden Fleece,"
and placed it under the protection of the Apostle; his knights wearing as a
badge the figure of a cross which is called St. Andrew's cross or the cross of
Burgundy. On the occasion of the Duke's marriage, January 10, 1433, the
order was consecrated to the Virgin Mary and the Apostle Andrew. This portion of the supposed cross is now at Tourney, in Belgium.

There are many improbable stories by frivolous authors; but the student of
history can collect from the church antiquaries authentic accounts concerning
the Apostles and their contemporaries. It is to be regretted that many of the
ancient ecclesiastical works to which reference is made by the early
writers, are not now extant, but many credible and unquestioned sayings have
been transmitted to us. Gregory, Bishop of Tours, reported that on the anniversary day of St. Andrew's martyrdom, there was wont to flow from his tomb,
"a most fragrant and precious oil, which according to its quantity denoted the
scarceness or plenty of the following year; and that the sick being anointed
with the oil were restored to their former health." It has been suggested that if
any semblance of truth attaches to the story, it was merely an "exhalation
and sweating forth at some time of those rare and costly perfumes and oint-

ment wherewith his body was embalmed " It was after this record that the body of the Apostle was removed to Constantinople by Constantine, in the year 337 and buried in the church which was built by him, and taken down some hundred years thereafter by Emperor Justinian, in order to its reparation, at which time the body of Andrew was found in a wooden coffin, and was again deposited in its proper place There is another record concerning the relics of St. Andrew, which states that when the city of Constantinople was captured by the French, Cardinal Peter of Capua, brought the relics of St Andrew from thence into Italy in 1210, and deposited them in the Cathedral of Amalphi

George Phranza, the last of the Byzantine historians, relates that when the Turks became masters of Constantinople, " Thomas the Despot," in going from Greece into Italy, carried with him the head of St Andrew and presented it to Pope Pius II in the year 1461, who allotted to him a monastery for his dwelling with a competent revenue

In the early ages the bones of the Saints were greatly venerated, especially those supposed to belong to an Apostle In addition to the disposition already named, it is stated that an arm bone of St Andrew was given to St Gregory the Great, by Tiberius II , another was deposited at Notre Dame at Paris , and other bones distribute i to certain churches and monasteries at Bordeaux, Rheims, Brussels, Orleans, Milan, Aix, and other places, which consider themselves enriched by their possession

It is represented that at the time Constantinople was taken, and the relics of St Andrew dispersed, a lively and intense enthusiasm for the Apostle was excited throughout all christendom The inspired account of St Andrew is confined to a few verses in the Gospels (—Matthew 4 18—10 2 , Mark 1 16—29—13 3—3 18 , Luke 5 2—6 14 , John 1 35, 40, 44—6 8—9—12 22 ,—Acts 1 13) The apparent discrepancy (in John 1 40, 41, with Matthew 4 18 and Mark 1 16.) where Andrew and Peter appear to have been called together is easily reconciled St John relates the first introduction of the brothers to Jesus , the other evangelists their formal call to follow Him in his ministry. In the catalogue of the Apostles, Andrew appears in Matthew (10 2, Luke 6 14,) as second, next after his brother Peter , but in Mark (3 18, Acts 1 13,) as fourth, following Peter, James and John, and in company with Philip, which is probably considered by some as his real place of dignity among the Apostles , but St Andrew, Scotland's illustrious patron—that grand and intrepid Apostle of the primitive church, stands pre-eminent as the " first born of the Apostolic quire " He had the distinguished honor of being the first disciple who came to Jesus—the first Christian believer—the first preacher of the Gospel under the new dispensation, and fully represented in himself the first complete embodiment of the Christian church in miniature

Nicephorus pretends on the authority of Euodius, who was St Peter's immediate successor in the See of Antioch for twenty-three years, and in whose time the disciples were first called Christians, " that of all the Apostles, Christ baptized none but Peter with his own hands , that Peter baptized Andrew and the two sons of Zebedee, and they the rest of the Apostles " Baronius, however, contends that the Epistle of Euodius was " altogether unknown to any of the ancients " There is a book bearing the title of ' The Acts of Andrew " as well the " Gospel of St Andrew," which by a decree of Pope Galasius, was declared apocryphal , and " The Acts of Andrew and Matthew," are also regarded as spurious Cardinal M'Closky in a sermon on the " Immaculate Conception," December 7, 1877, refers to " the earliest liturgies of the church, in the liturgy of St James and in that of St Andrew."

Each of the Apostles had his mission Continuing with the Saviour until the crucifixion, the world was so divided after the day of Pentecost, as to

give to each of them his respective field of labor, and they then entered upon
their public ministry.   Biographical brevity is characteristic of New Testament
history   The record of each of the Apostles and early disciples is limited, and
only elaborated in the case of Peter and Paul, one representing the circumcision,
and called the "Apostle of the Circumcision," the other the uncircumcision, to
whom, (according to Gal 2 7,) "the Gospel of the uncircumcision was com-
mitted."

Andrew in his first following of Jesus, was not so constant in his attendance
as to prevent him from continuing his occupation as a fisherman   He had
stood with John when he bore testimony to the divinity, the humanity and the
office of One among them "whom they knew not"   He was with him at the
Ford of Bethabara, when he announced 'Behold the Lamb of God," and
when he bore record "This is the Son of God"   After which Andrew "findeth
his own brother Simon," saying unto him, "We have found the Messiah"
When Andrew's constant presence became necessary, he was formally called
by the Master and accompanied Him in his journeyings, and was an eye and
ear witness of His wonderful acts and sayings, saw His miracles, listened to
His teachings, heard His discourses, and conversed freely with Him, thereby
becoming thoroughly prepared for the great work which was graciously assigned
to him

In the calling to the Apostleship of Matthew, James and John, Peter and
Andrew are specially and prominently mentioned, while the circumstances
attending the calling of the other seven are not recorded   On account of the
priority assigned to Peter, it has been supposed that he was the oldest of the
Apostles, but there are writers who consider Andrew to have been older
than his brother. He is generally represented as younger   There is no
scriptural authority on the subject

St. Andrew was styled by the Cretes the "First Called"   He was emphati-
cally the "First Missionary," for when St John the Baptist saluted the Saviour,
Andrew followed Him, and "abode with Him that day"   Immediately on being
convinced that Jesus was the Messiah, he started to communicate the glad
tidings to others, and persuaded them to come and see for themselves   The
promptness and alacrity of the Apostle has been suggestive, for in some cities,
particularly in Montreal and New York, I have read of "Philip and Andrew
Societies," whose specific work is to bring persons to the Saviour   These
brotherhoods connected with local churches are active and aggressive, and are
appropriately named, because Philip and Andrew early exemplified a true
missionary spirit

The names of Philip and Andrew are intimately associated with
the Greeks who desired to "See Jesus," which occurred during the last days
of the Saviour's ministry in the courts of the Temple, in the presence of
Andrew and these Greeks who had come to Jerusalem to the feast of the Passover, and were called "proselytes of the gate or covenant"   The Father declared the third time His love for the Beloved Son, by AN AUDIBLE VOICE, thus
convincing the Greeks, who were to be the first fruits of the Gentiles, that
Jesus was the Messiah   Andrew having been a disciple of St John the
Baptist before the advent of Jesus as a public teacher, and probably a mem-
ber of the sect to which John belonged—the Essenian, a Jewish sect of mystics,
ascetics,—may "account for the learning" and ability which he subsequently
exhibited in his public ministry

THE THISTLE

The Thistle is the National emblem of Scotland, and evoked from her illustrious bard the tribute —

" The rough burr thistle spreading wide
Among the bearded bear,
I turned the weeder—clips aside,
An spar d the symbol dear. '

The Scottish order of Knighthood known as " The Thistle," has for its principal decoration, a gold collar composed of sixteen thistles, interlaced with
sprigs of rue , to which are suspended a small image of St Andrew, and this
Saint's cross of silver   In the centre of this is a thistle surrounded by the
motto of the Order, from which emanate silver rays forming a star   The
motto of the Order, as also that of Scotland, is a Latin inscription, " *Nemo me
impune lacessit*,"—no one insults me with impunity   The institution of the
order in honor of St Andrew, is attributed by the Scots to King Achaias in
the 8th century, in memory of an appearance in the heavens of a bright cross
resembling that whereon St Andrew suffered martyrdom,—seen by Achaias
the night before he gained a victory over Athelstan, King of Northumberland,
the first who called himself King of England   He died in 940.   The introduction of the order has also been attributed to the same King (Achaias), as
commemorative of a famous league of amity he formed with Charlemagne
(Charles the Great), King of France, he having selected as a badge "The
Thistle and the Rue "   It has also been suggested that Charles VII, of France,
who reigned 1403–1461, having received great assistance from Scotland, renewed the league of amity which had been entered into with Achaias,
the 65th King of Scotland, who had died in 809   Authors are divided as to the
origin of the order , but it was no doubt instituted in 787 , restored about 1540,
by James V, of Scotland, who was "the handsomest and most chivalrous
Prince of his times," revived May 29, 1687, by King James VII (II
of England) , and reestablished by Queen Anne, December 31, 1703   This
order also called the Order of St Andrew , was accessable only to the
Peers   It dates at least from the time of King Robert II, 1370–90, whose
coin bore the cross and image of St Andrew   The order as a regular ' organized knightly fraternity," is conceded as existing in the reign of King James
VII, in 1687   By a statute passed in May, 1827, the order consists of the
sovereign and sixteen knights   It is contended by some that the badge of the
Thistle may not have been worn before the reign of James III, and was
not probably connected with any distinct order of knighthood previous to
James V. 1540   If the Thistle and the Rue, as one writer claims, were
once symbols of two different orders, one " The Thistle," with the present
motto , the other " The Garland of Rue," it is certain that from the collars of
both hung one and the same jewel, the figure of St Andrew bearing his
cross   The Thistles, which no one could touch without being hurt, was in
the badge significantly associated with the Rue, the antidote for poison

The Andrew cross is worn in their hats, by the people of Scotland, on the
day of the feast of the Saint   It consists of blue and white ribbons disposed
with a cross, and is intended as a commemoration of his crucification   I have
before me seven ancient copper coins with three thistles on one stalk, one
bearing date 1678, another 1692   The other five pieces are older but without
date, or the dates cannot be deciphered, and are quite crude and irregular in
workmanship, having been made and stamped by hand, machinery not being
used in coining at the early period they were made   One of the gold coins
issued by King Robert II, 1371–90, was called " St Andrew's," and bore the
image of the Saint on his cross   Another was issued with only a St Andrew
cross   The " St Andrew's " of Robert III, 1390–1406, has the figure of the
Saint on the cross   The " St Andrew's Half," differs by representing the
Saint with his arms extended, but without the cross   The gold coinage of

James I dates from 1433, and has on the reverse side a small St Andrew's cross In 1451, the gold issue of "St Andrew's" and its half (James II), bore on the reverse of each a figure of the Saint The gold coinage of James III, 1460–67, consisted of a "St Andrew's" and the "St Andrew's Half" In 1468, the Billon-Plack and half Plack appeared, bearing a St Andrew's cross in centre on the reverse side In 1488, James IV, the "St Andrew's" bore the image of the Saint, with a glory round his head, together with his cross which reached to the outer edge of the coin In the last coinage of James IV, 1512, appeared the Billon Plack, representing the Saint and cross in each quarter In the second issue of the same year, the Saint and cross appear in the centre In 1677–81, some of the coins were adorned with a St Andrew's cross passing through a crown, and have the thistle design Other coins might be mentioned with somewhat similar devices Towards the close of the last century, a large number of copper tokens were circulated as coin, by private corporations and individuals One of the Edinburgh half penny tokens represents St Andrew carrying his cross in front of him, with the erect thistle on either side It had also on the rim the motto of the order The Russian quarter roubles of Peter the Great, of 1701, had an eagle with a St Andrew's cross around his neck The roubles of 1723 had the Grand Ribbon of the order of St. Andrew, of 1724, the Star of the order of St Andrew Peter the Great died in 1725, and his widow Catharine I, had new designs, and among the adornments, the broad Ribbon and Star of St Andrew In 1731–41, on the half roubles of Anna, the broad ribbon of the order of St Andrew is worn by the figure in armor In 1741, a Russian coin has a small bust, draped, and wearing the ribbon and badge of St Andrew These references to coins may not be deemed pertinent to our subject, but being interesting in connection with the Saint, may be regarded as permissible

There is a tradition that "The Thistle" was first suggested as the national emblem, by a circumstance which occurred during the invasion of Scotland by the Norseman (Danes) Meditating the surprise of a Scottish camp, at night, and while the main force were halting, a spy in endeavoring to discover the undefended points, stepped with bare feet upon a thistle, which caused such pain that his loud and involuntary exclamation prevented a surprise by arousing the "unsuspecting Scots," who immediately attacked and repulsed the invaders and obtained a complete victory The Scotch thistle (*crucus acaulies*) was recognized as instrumental to their success, and has since been regarded as the heraldic badge of Scotland

The "Wisconsin Historical Collections" (vol 4,) refer to a relic of the Scotch rebellion, which is deposited in the rooms of the Historical Society of that State, at Madison It is 'a portion of an old red silk flag, bearing date in gilt figures 1719, which is four years later than the Scotch rebellion of 1715," "also the Scotch Thistle in gilt and the Latin motto of the Order of the Thistle or Knights of St Andrew" It was obtained from a Captain Clarkson, of Ceresco, Wisconsin, a lineal descendent of its original owner By distinct tradition of the family through whom the ancient flag has been handed down, it was used in the memorable Scottish rebellion of 1745, and was in the fatal defeat of Prince Charlie at Culloden, soon after which its early possessors—the Clarkson family—migrated to New England, bringing this interesting relic with them There is also recorded in Brewster's "Rambles about Portsmouth," New Hampshire, (vol I), an interesting account of two brothers, Andrew and John Clarkson, who occupied a spacious old framed house with gambrel-roof which I well remember to have frequently shunned in my boyhood days as haunted In 1835, the grand old mansion, long unoccupied, was demolished The Clarksons are represented as natives of Scotland, and men of distinction

Andrew "enlisted under the banner of the Pretender, and was an ensign in his army." He "came to this country in the year 1717, and brought with him the colors belonging to his company." Whether or not the two accounts refer to the same flag, I am unable to determine. A discrepency in dates exists ; but this might occur in statements derived from traditional and not published sources

Masonry honors St. Andrew, records his name in her calendar and observes St. Andrew's day. Many lodges bear his appellation, and none more worthy than the "Lodge of St. Andrew," of Boston, Mass., which obtained its charter from the Grand Lodge of Masons in Scotland, November 30, 1756, and is noted for its excellency of membership, munificence in charity, and proficiency in Masonry. Enrolled upon its scroll of membership are the names of many men of renown, Joseph Warren and Paul Revere being conspicuous. The twenty-ninth degree in the Ancient and Accepted Scottish Rite of Free Masonry, is known as the order of "Grand Scottish Knight of St. Andrew." The banner of the order is white, fringed with gold, with a St. Andrew's cross in green on each side. The dress of the knights, in part, is a crimson robe, having embroidered on the left breast a large white St. Andrew's cross ; the jewels, a St. Andrew's cross of gold, with a large emerald in the centre, surmounted by the helmet of a knight, and with a thistle of gold between the arms at the bottom. The lessons of the order teach humility, patience and self-denial as essential virtues ; also, charity, clemency and generosity, as well as virtue, truth and honor, as most excellent qualities which should characterize all so distinguished in Masonry as the "Grand Scottish Knights of St. Andrew." The order was established by King Robert Bruce, in 1314, and was first composed of persecuted brethren of the order of the 'House of the Temple at Jerusalem," "The Knighthood of the Temple of Solomon" or of "The Knights of the Temple," was established in 1118, and declared heretical by Pope Clement V, at the instance of Philip the Fair of France, in 1307. The members of the order in that country, were imprisoned, many executed, more tortured and all impoverished. In most of the European States their property had been confiscated, and their leaders incarcerated, which caused the persecuted brethren to leave their homes and lay aside the garb of the "Temple." In England, King Edward proscribed them, unless they entered the Perfectories of the Knights of St. John of Jerusalem or of the Hospital. In Scotland, however, they found protection, and joined the army with which King Robert Bruce resisted the invasion of Scotland by Edward II, of England. The battle of Bannockburn was fought on the 24th of June, 1314. In recognition of the heroic aid of the Templars on that memorable day, Bruce created, and then received them into, the Order of St. Andrew-du-chardon (of the thistle), of Scotland, which was afterwards annexed to the degree of the Rite of Herodum, which concealed the real name of the order "The Holy House of the Temple at Jerusalem." When the Ancient and Accepted Scottish Rite was finally organized by those in possession of the degree of the Rites of Herodum and Perfection and other Rites, and detached degrees that had been from time to time established in Scotland, France, Germany and elsewhere, the order of "Grand Scottish Knights of St. Andrew," became the twenty-ninth of the new Rite formed by selecting from the different rites and observances, seven degrees in addition to the twenty-five of Perfection, and created the thirty-third as the supreme and last degree to rule the whole.

The Standard of Great Britain is formed by the union of the three crosses of St. George, St. Andrew and St. Patrick. It is called the great Union Flag of the Empire of Great Britain. It is recorded that the flag called the Great Union, raised by Washington at Cambridge, Mass., January 2, 1776, consisted of thirteen alternate red and white stripes of the present flag of the United States, with the crosses of St George and St Andrew emblazoned on the blue canton in place of the stars

Many churches likewise bear the manly and exalted name of St Andrew Near by my own New Hampshire home, there stands a little church, not far from the ragged headlands , and as the prayers of its worshippers ascend on high, the grand old ocean, that great wonder of the Creator, beats its ceaseless monotone as it laves the pebbly beach and thunders along the rocky coast   To this sacred edifice, recently erected, has been given the appropriate name of "St Andrew's by the Sea "

At Madrid, in the Museo-del-Rey, are collected forty-five pictures by Murillo, the celebrated Spanish painter (1618–1682) , one deserving special mention, is the Martyrdom of St Andrew   It is described as " painted in small proportions, and is one of the best of the ærial style , a silver tint, which seems showered down from heaven by the angels holding out the palm of immortality to St Andrew, who is being crucified, pervades every object, softens the outlines, harmonizes the tints and gives the whole scene a cloudy and fantastic appearance, which is full of charms "   In the collection of Mr Miles at Leigh Court, is another painting by Murillo exhibiting St Andrew suspended on a high cross, formed of the trunks of trees laid transversly   This is described as a work of great beauty and very effective   I would here remark that all authorities are not agreed concerning the form of the cross   One says it was an Olive tree and not a cross formed of plank   "The Martyrdom of St Andrew " and the Saint preaching the Gospel, by Jaun-de-Roelas, are also mentioned as splendid productions of art   In the Hampton Court Palace, were deposited seven cartoons which were brought to England by K'ng Charles the First from Brussels, in 1629, at the suggestion of Rubens, the distinguished Flemish painter   They were the composition of "Raphael the Divine," and prepared by that Prince of Painters, who is recognized as without a rival   He designed in the years 1513–16, twenty five scenes executed in colors, representing Gospel subjects, which were copied at Brussels, by being woven in tapestry fourteen to eighteen feet in length and twelve in height   Several are preserved at the Vatican at Rome, and in the European courts   Among the number formerly at Hampton Palace, but now exhibited at South Kensington Museum, is one representing " Christ calling Peter and Andrew," but more generally known as "The Miraculous Draught of Fishes " in which the Saviour, Peter and Andrew are in one boat, and Zebedee and his sons James and John in another   They are the prominent and absorbing features of the sketch, which is particularly distinguished as having all of Raphael's characteristics of " simplicity, perspicuity, emphatic expression and clear developement of the story it illustrates "   In Leonardo-de-Vinci's celebrated picture of the Lord's supper, which is painted upon the walls of the Refectory of the Dominican Convent at Milan, Italy, and was completed in 1492, the position of St Andrew is next to Phi'ip, who is near the end of the table earnestly looking at Jesus   Andrew is seated with his elbows resting upon the table

In the ancient Greek types and in the old Mosaics, St Andrew is represented as aged, with flowing white hair and beard, and is distinguished by the transversed cross   Since the fourteenth century, in the devotional pictures in which St Andrew figures, he is represented as a very old man, his hair and beard silver white, long, loose and flowing , and in general the beard is divided   He leans upon his cross, and holds the Gospel in his right hand   "St Andrew adoring his cross," by Andrea Sacchi, which is in the gallery of the Vatican at Rome, is remarkable "for its simplicity and fine expression "   Guido painted in fresco in the Chapel of St. Andrea in the Church of St Gregorio, at Rome, "St.

Andrew's Adoration of his Cross," and on the opposite wall Domenichius paint-ed the "Flagellation of St Andrew" He also painted the same subject in the Church of St Andrea-della-Valle, in somewhat different style, choosing another "moment of the torture," and in the same church the crucifixtion of the Saint and his apotheosis surmounting the whole Correggio, the great Italian painter, secured additional lustre to his name by his matchless genius he displayed in delineating the Apostles "The calling of St Peter and St Andrew" by Masaccio and Guido, 1407–43, now in the church of the Car-melites at Florence, are very celebrated "The Communion of the Apostles," by Ribera an Italian artist at Naples, in San Mantino, is also considered a master-piece Cespeda's painting of "The Last Supper," has a marked reputa-tion In the mediæval pictures, the Apostles are represented by distinc-tive badges or appendages, as Peter with the keys, James the son of Zebedee (James the Greater) with a pilgrim's staff and a gourd bottle, John with a cup and a winged serpent flying out of it, Philip with a long staff shaped like a cross, Bartholomew with a knife, Thomas with a lance, Matthew with a hatchet, James the son of Alpheus (James the Less) with a fuller's pole, Lebbeas whose surname was Thaddeus (St Jude) with a club, Simon the Canaanite with a saw, Matthias with a battle-axe, St Paul with a sword St Andrew is represented in all pictures and sculptures with a cross

I have thus enumerated a few of the famous paintings by the great masters in which St Andrew is a prominent figure In the collections of paintings, mosaics, engravings, sculpture, carvings and castings, which are extensively dis-persed over Europe and constitute one of the greatest attractions of its lead-ing cities, there are a large number in which he is represented grouped with other Saints, or isolated and alone with his cross I have had the privilege of seeing most of these notable works of art to which I have referred.

In considering the life and character of St Andrew, alike renowned in sacred and profane history, I have briefly recounted the prominent events of his Apostleship, the fortitude and fidelity which characterized his mission, and the patience and heroism exhibited at his martyrdom , the respect paid to his memory by the potentates of earth , the reverence of a nation whose Patron he became , the veneration of communities incorporated by his name ; and the tributes of genius in symbolizing through the medium of form the qualities which distinguished him He has been delineated on the canvas, sculptured in marble, wrought in mosaics, woven in tapestry, emblematized on coin, carved in wood, engraved on stone and cast in bronze Temples of piety, houses of mercy, and institutions of learning, have been dedicated to his memory. Societies, religious and secular, perpetuate his name—a name which must ever be sacred in Christian annals , illustrious on the martyrs' scroll , conspicu-ous in the orders instituted by men , and inestimably dear to the Christian heart as an eminent exemplar of a divinely religious faith His name, "Written in the Book of Life," shines "as the brightness of the firnament," and will endure the stars forever and ever "

When I commenced to note my thoughts and examine my collections relat-ing to the illustrious Saint whose name we all revere, I had no purpose of writing so extended a sketch It has been collated from scriptural and histori-cal sources, as well as traditional and legendary records I have not attempted to question the authenticity of any of the statements I have consulted as to the history of St Andrew or to discredit in the least whatever has been ascribed to him, but have given such scriptural and historical facts, as well as traditional reports, as I have been able to gather from the materials within my reach relat-ing to him , and I shall now leave it to you to discriminate between what is known to be historical truth and what may be mere fiction Having been deeply interested in considering the subject and in the preparation of this sketch, I trust I have been successful in enlisting your interest, without exhausting your patience by its recital, and that it may have imparted some information which will be new concerning St Andrew the Apostle, and the patron Saint of . Scotland

Milton Keynes UK
Ingram Content Group UK Ltd.
UKHW020959240124
436589UK00004B/71

9 781019 766880